This Book Belongs To:

Date Started

Date Finished

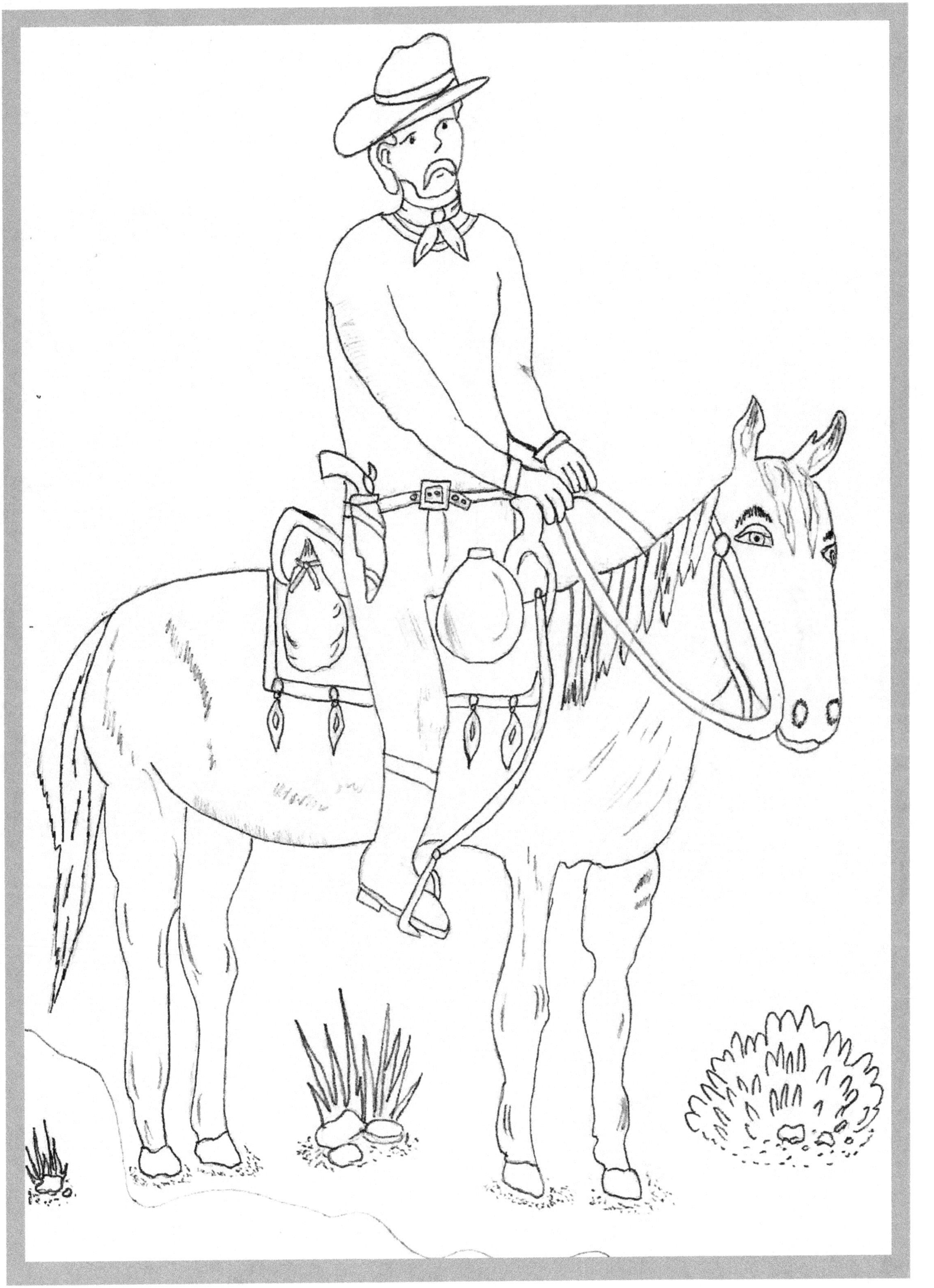

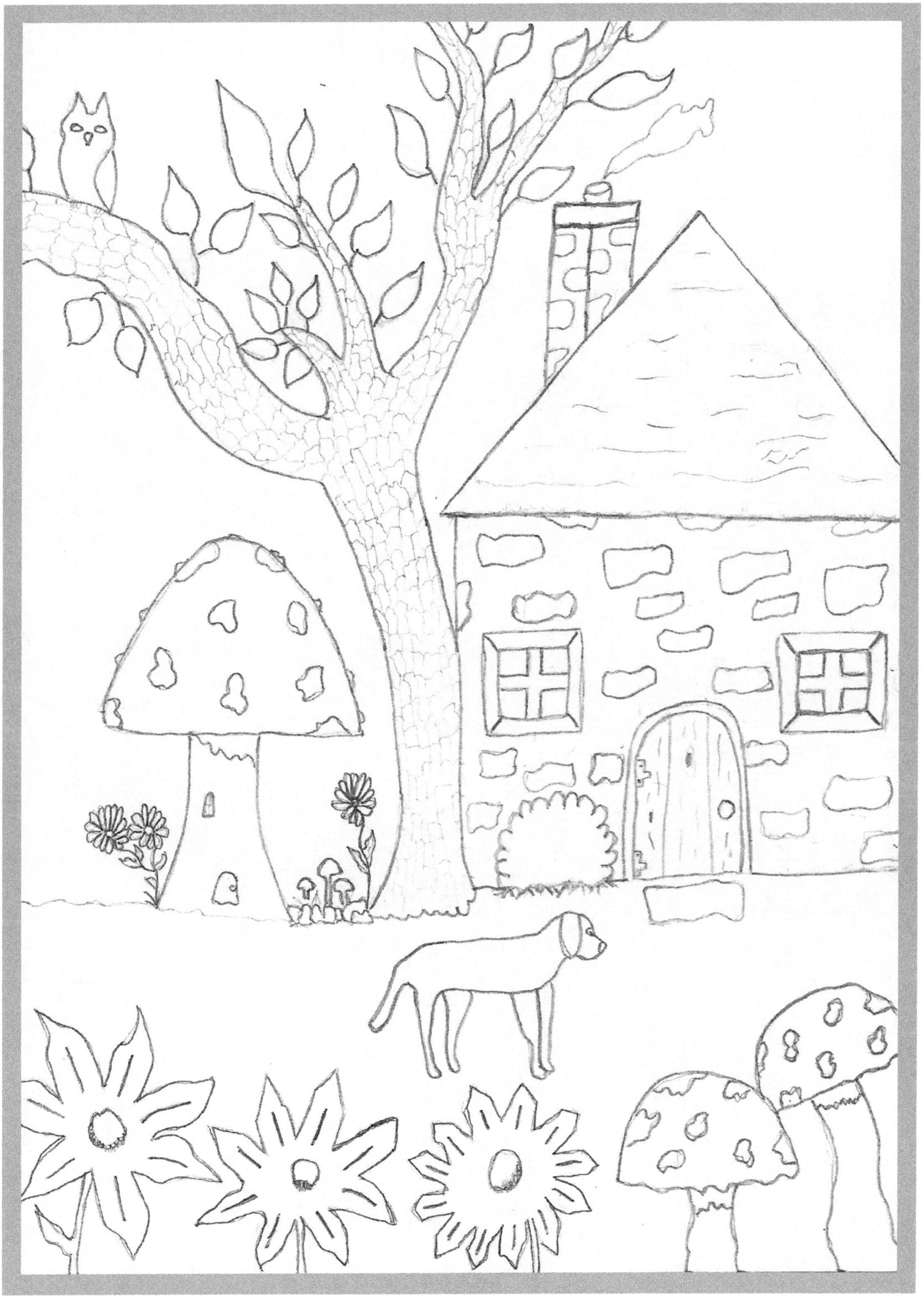

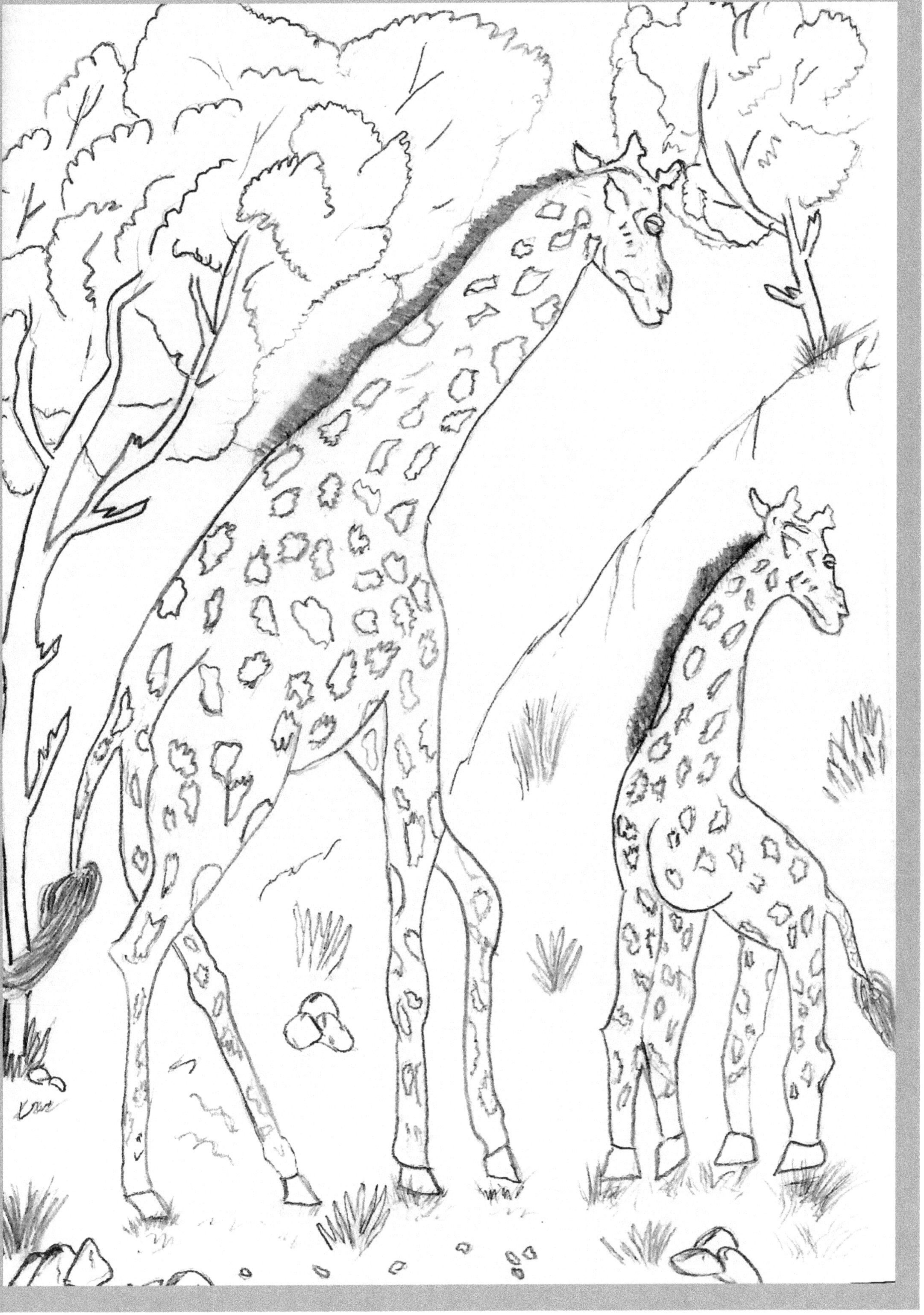

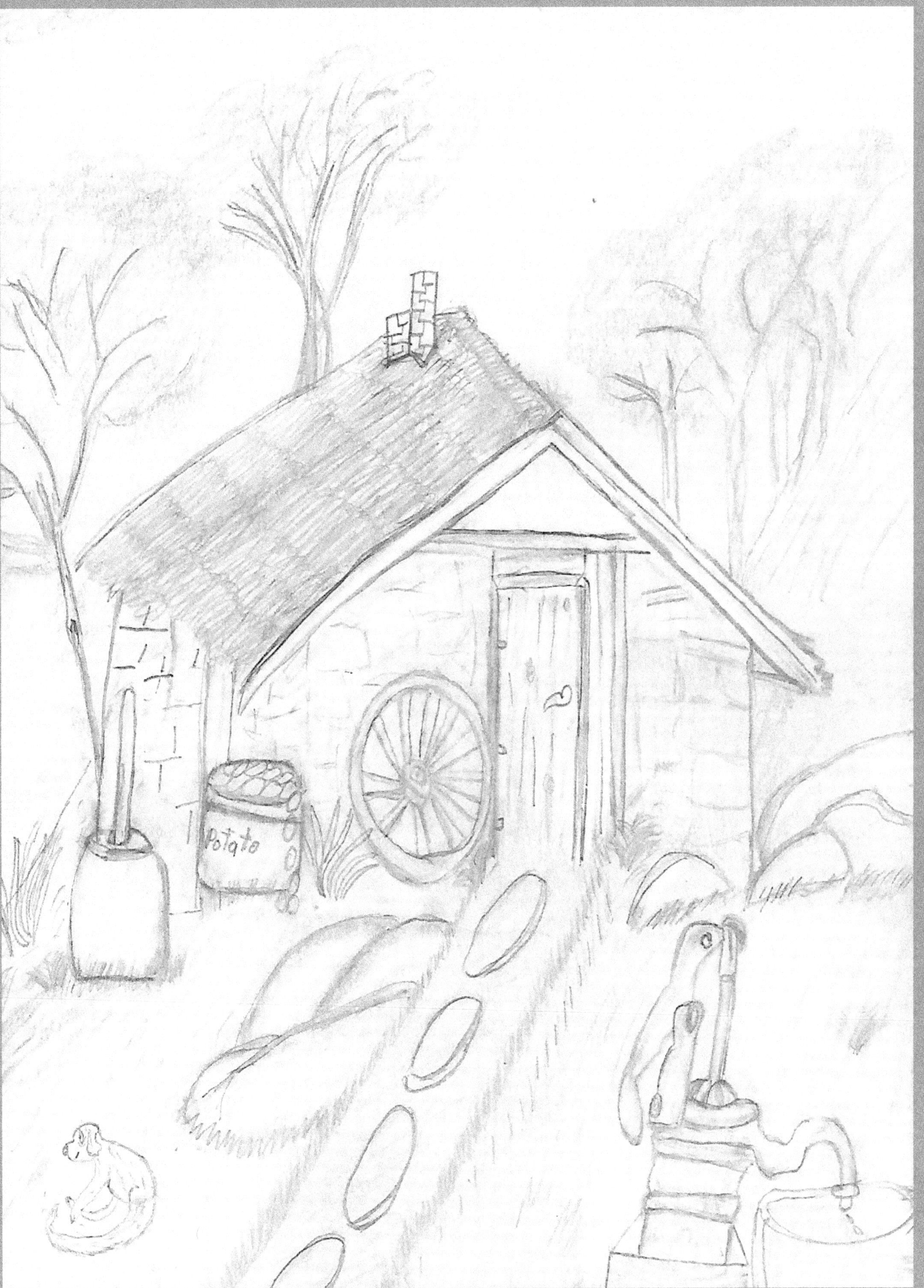
Potato

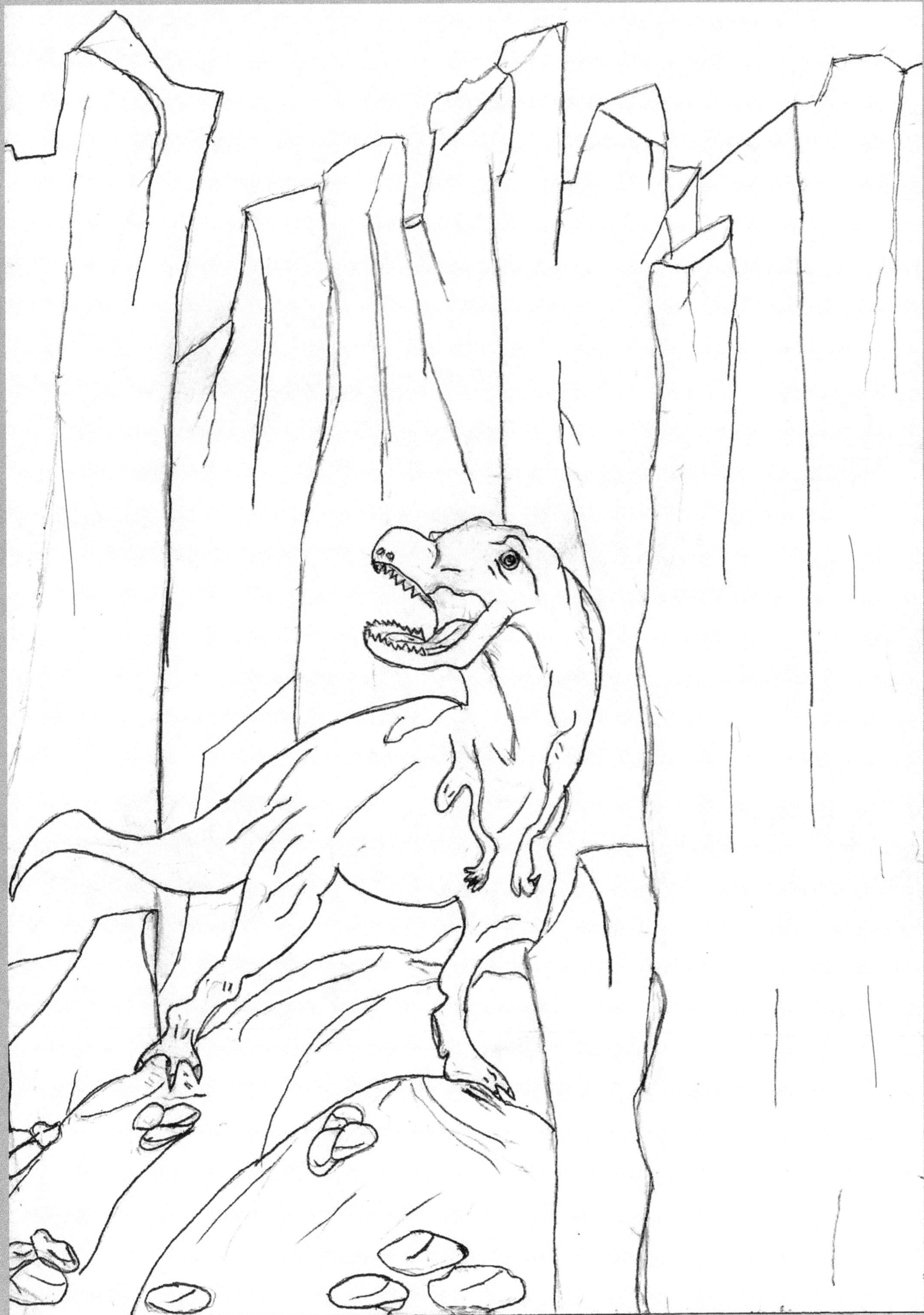

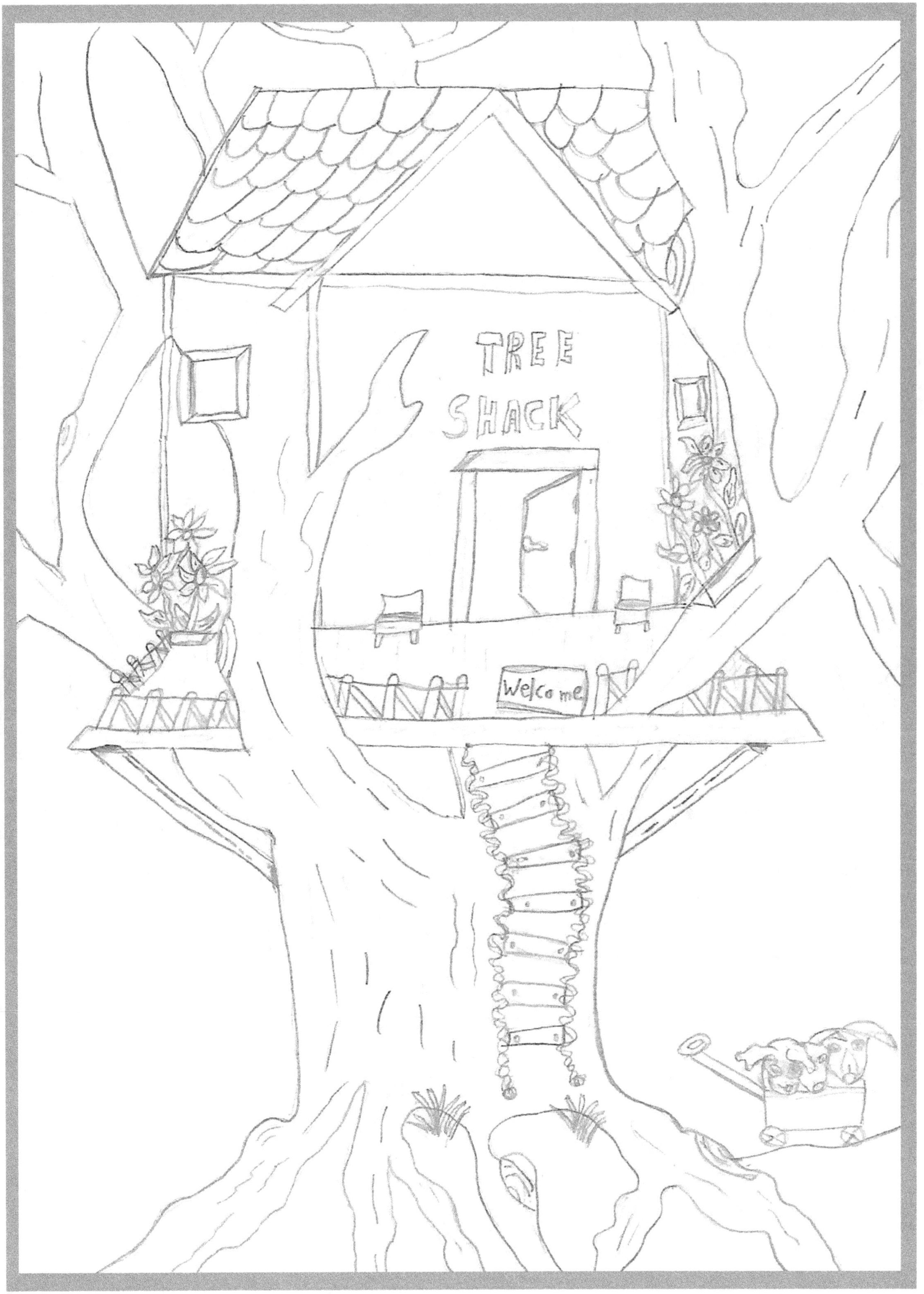
TREE
SHACK
Welcome

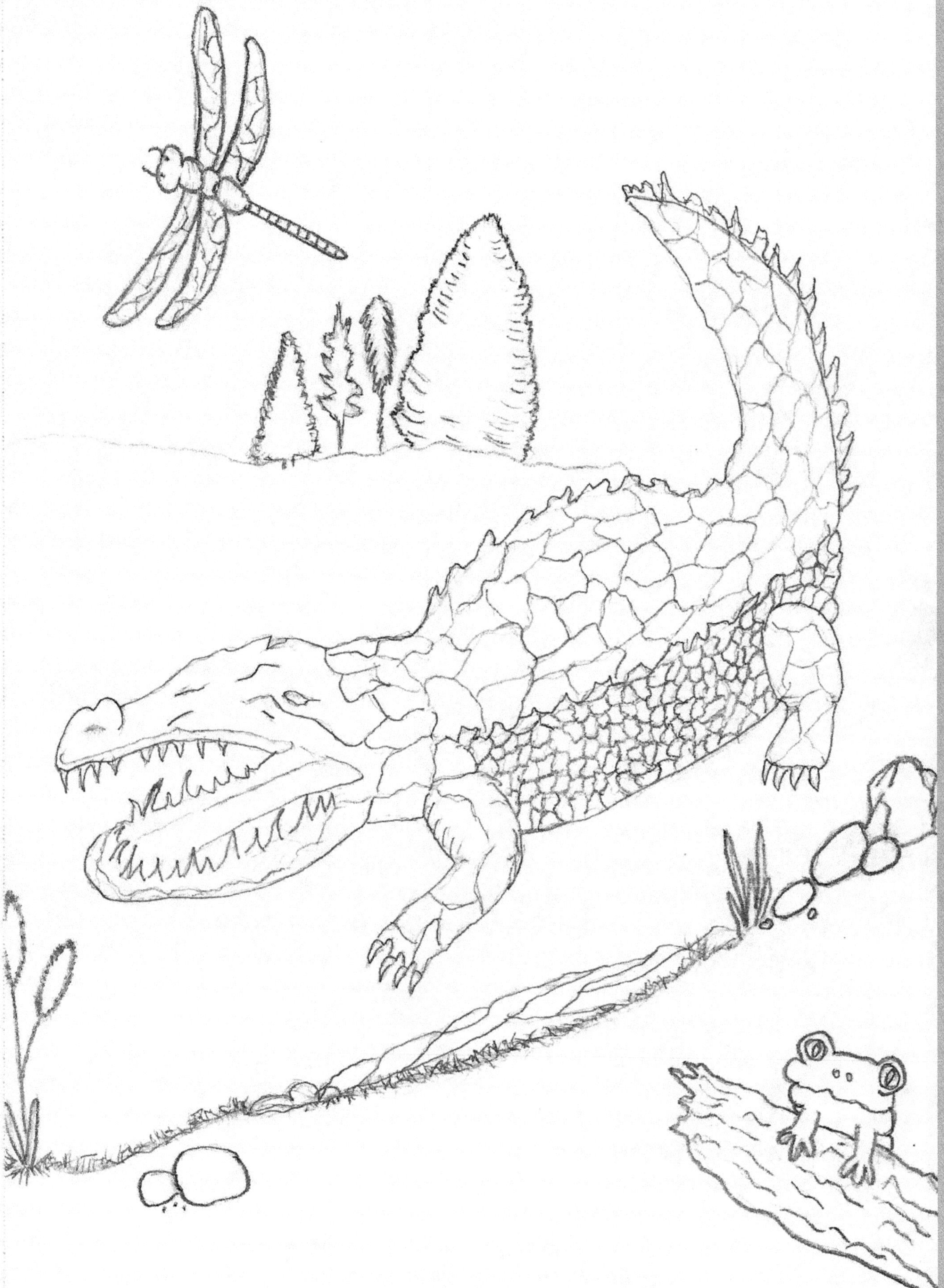

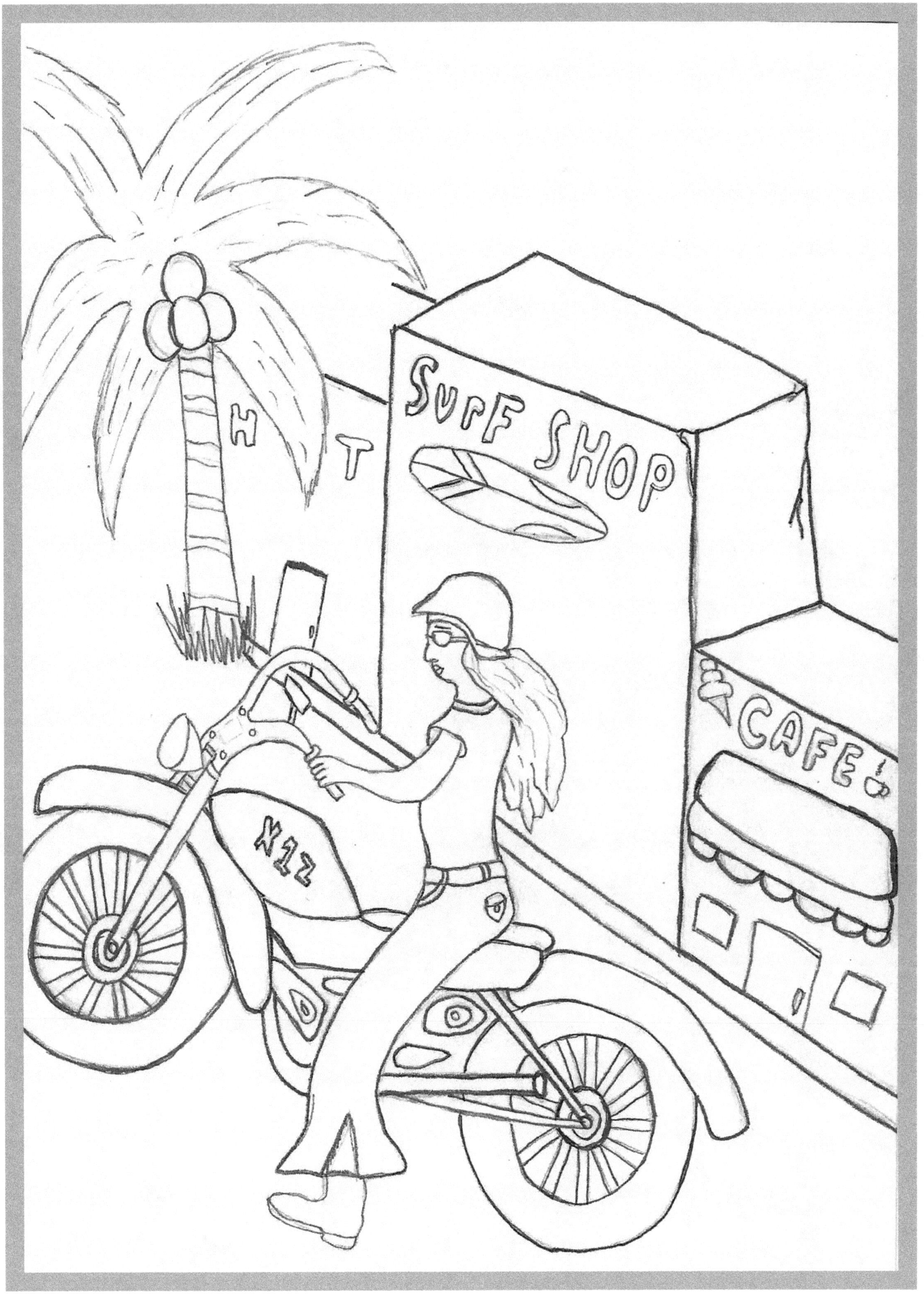

Surf SHOP
CAFE
X12

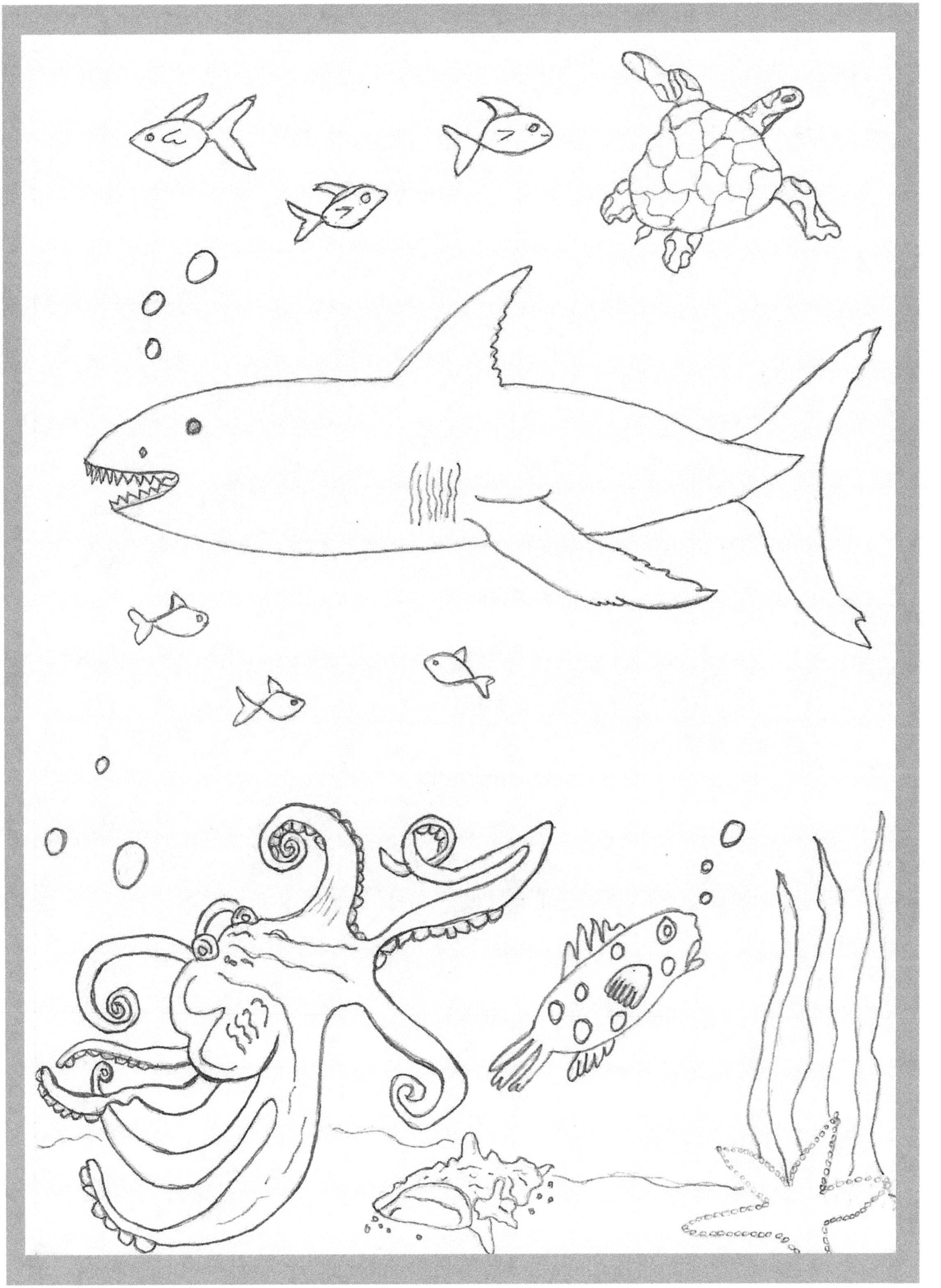

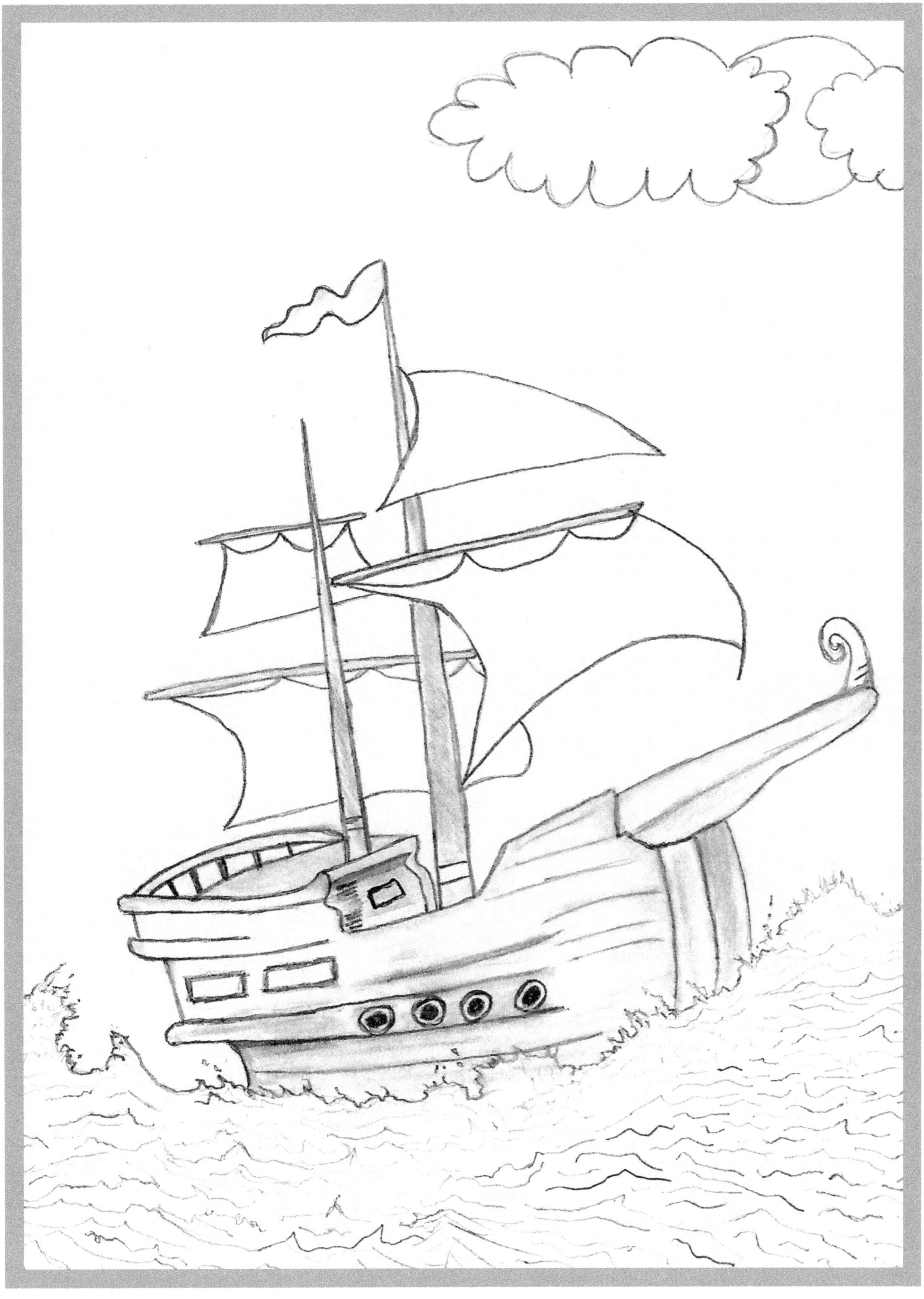

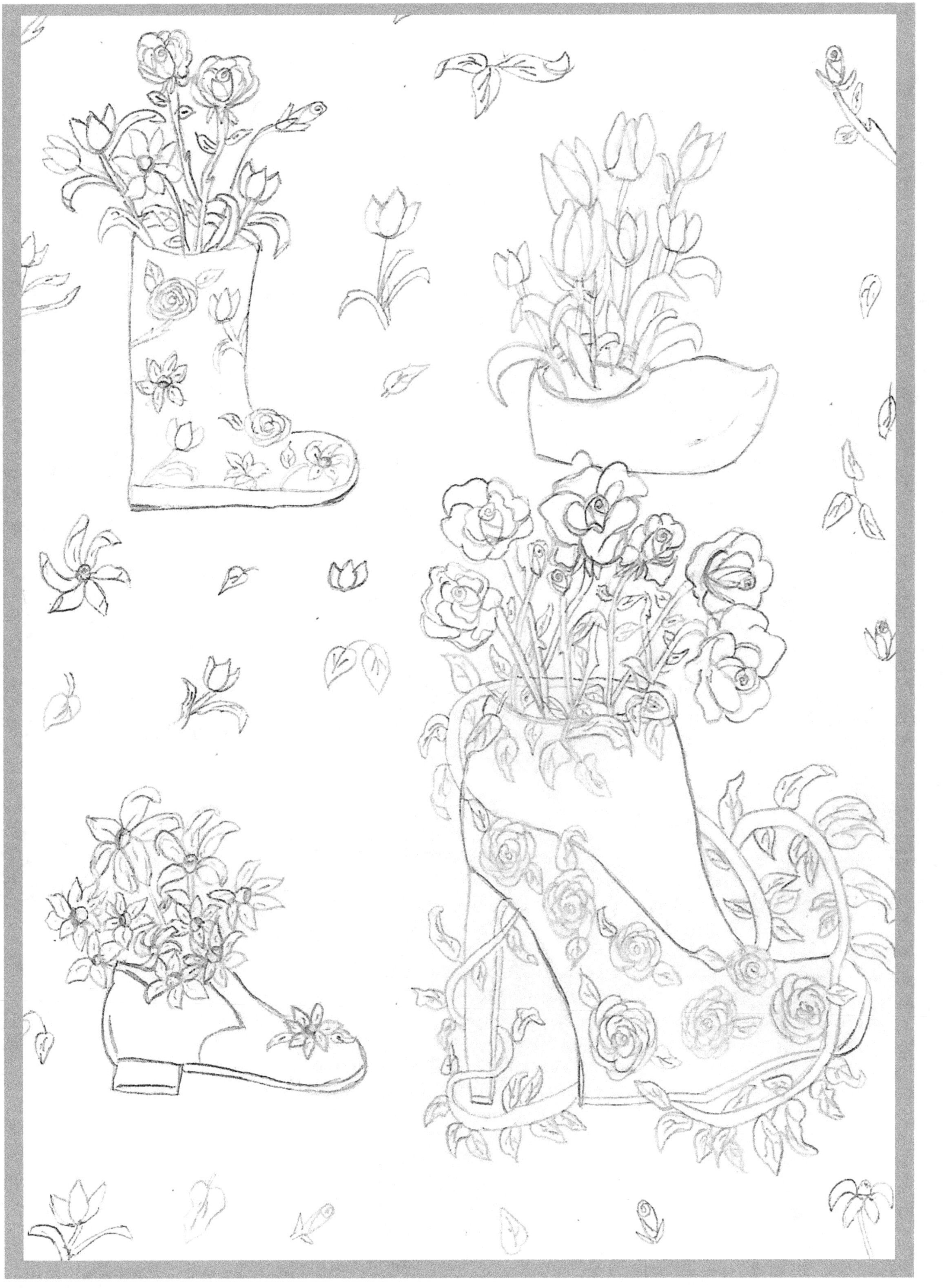

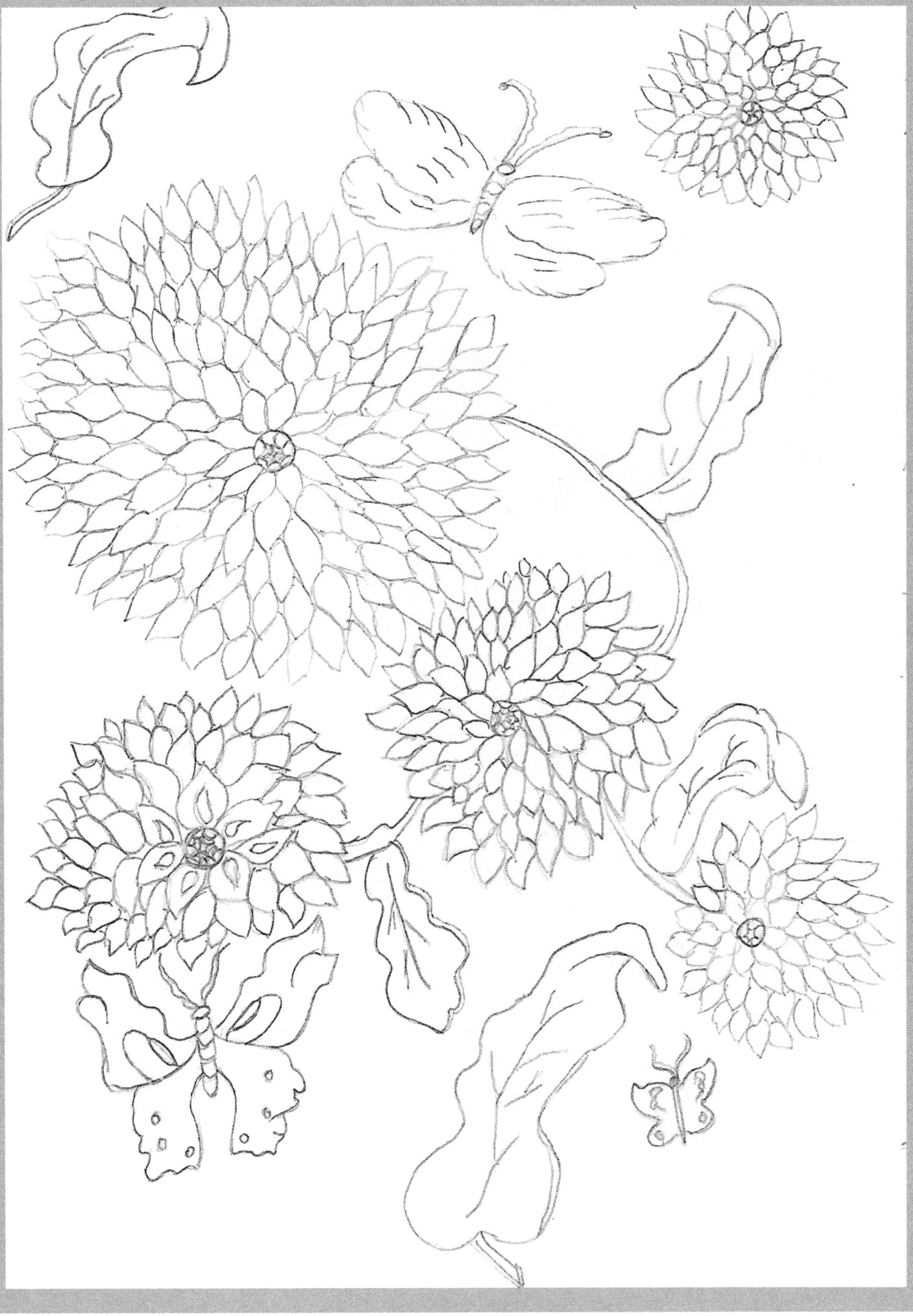

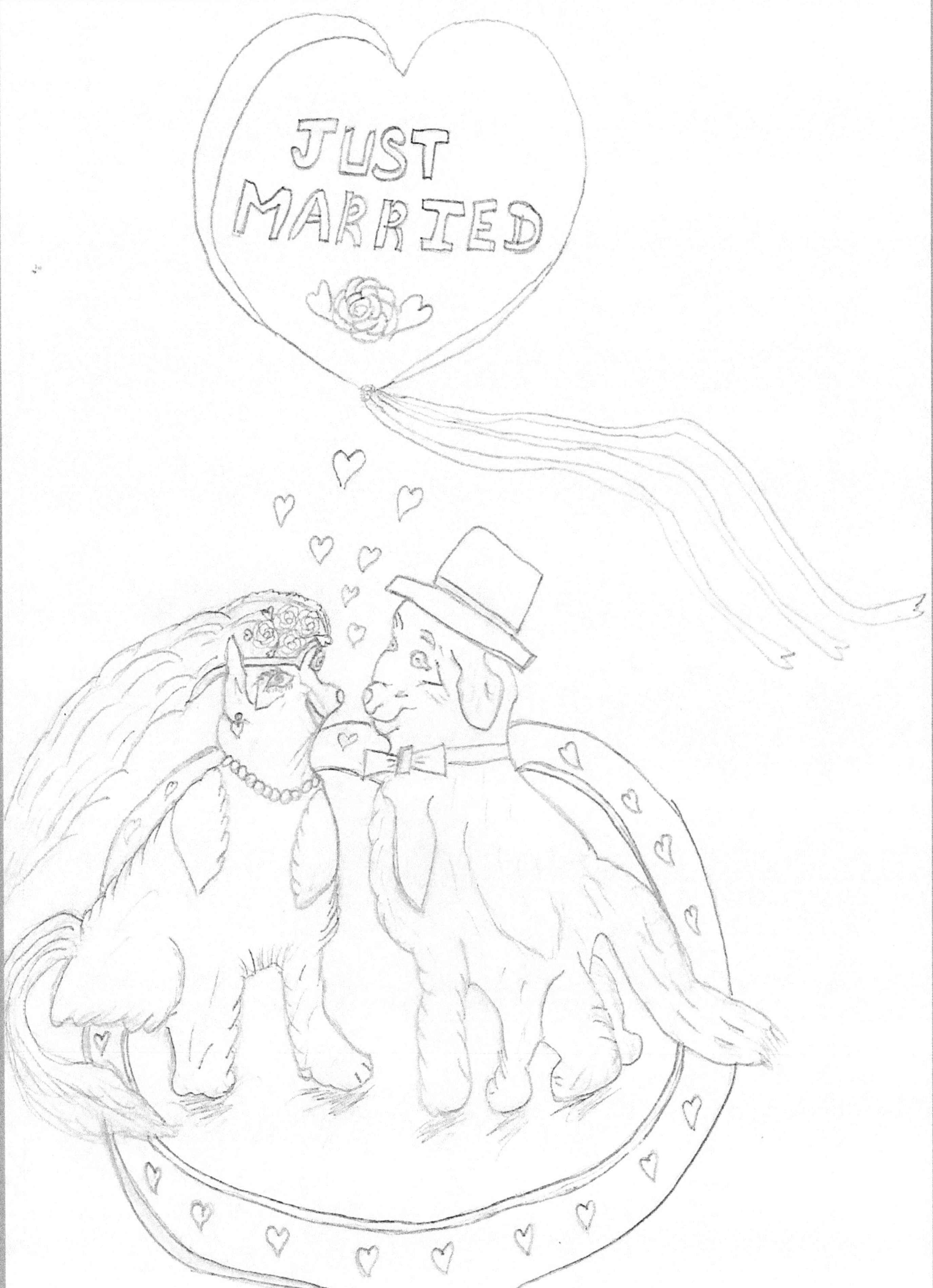
JUST MARRIED

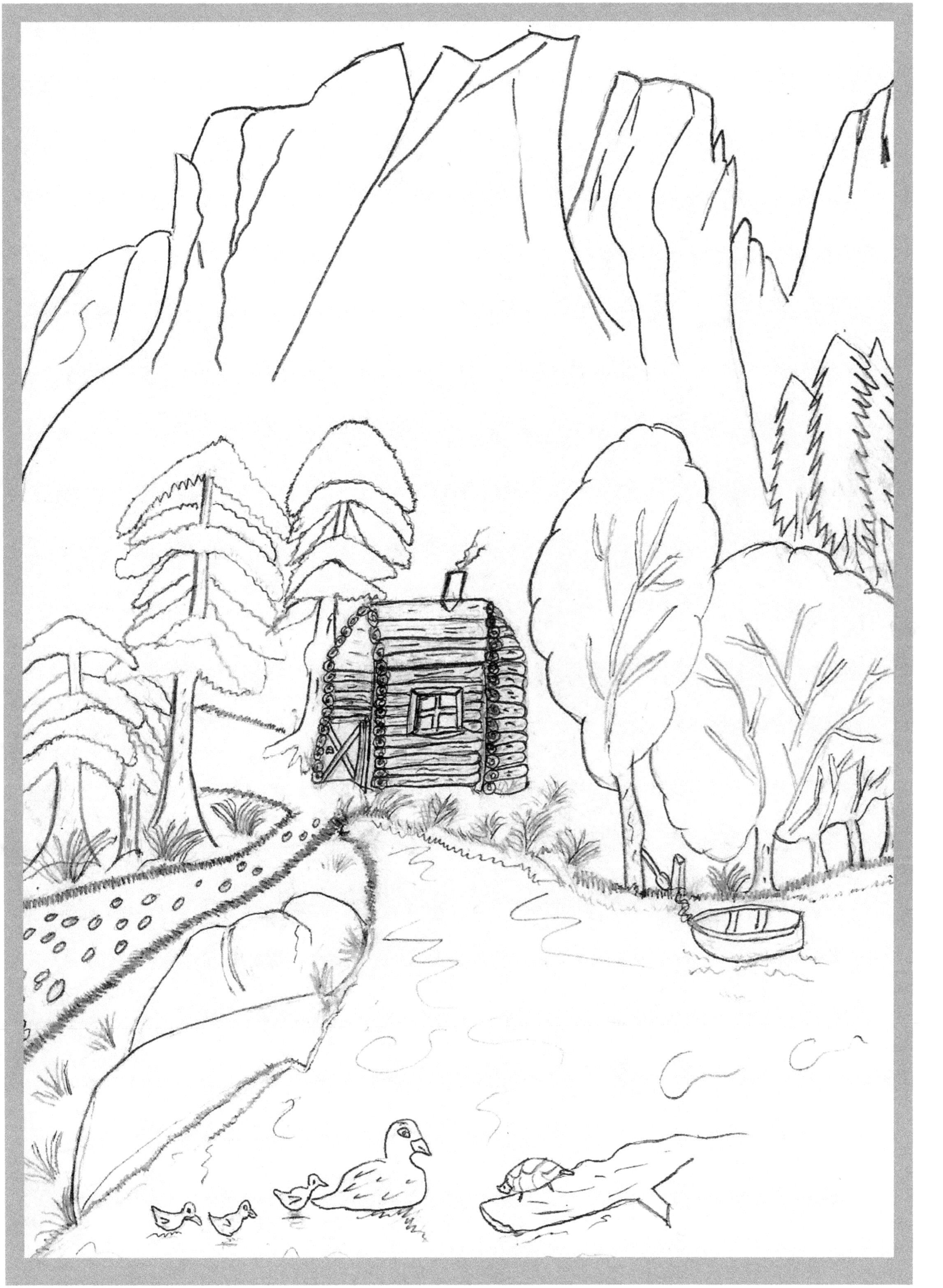

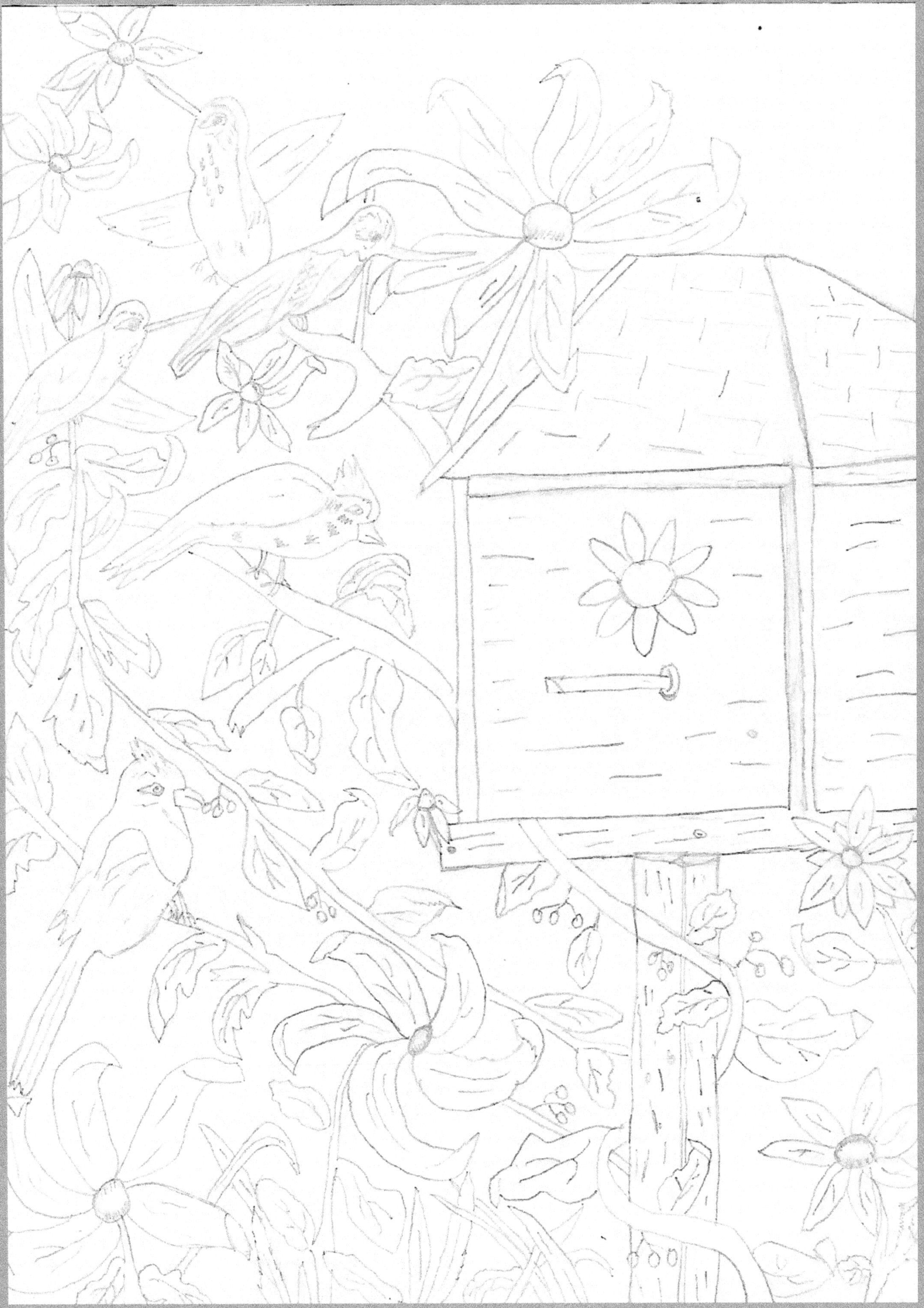

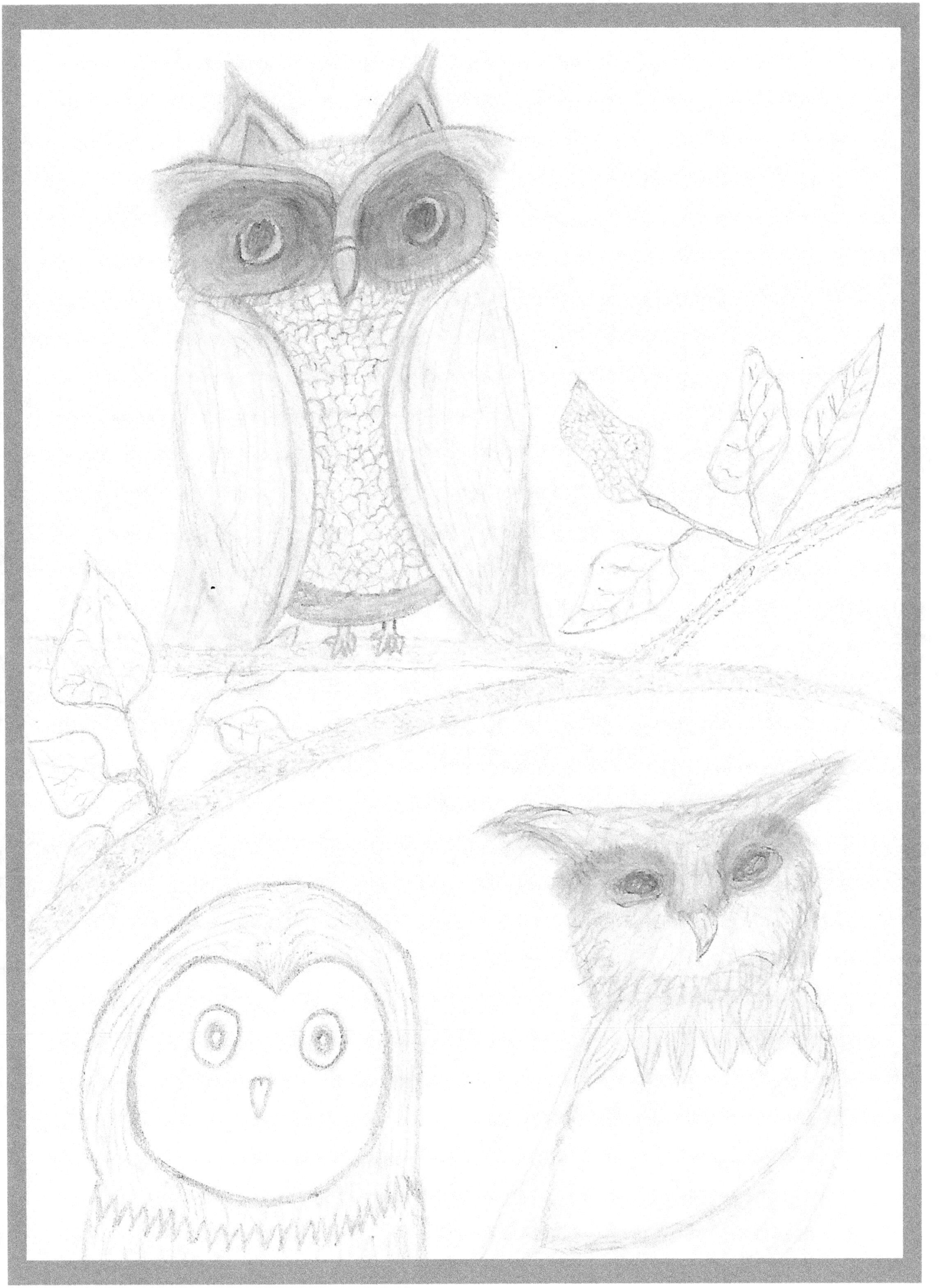

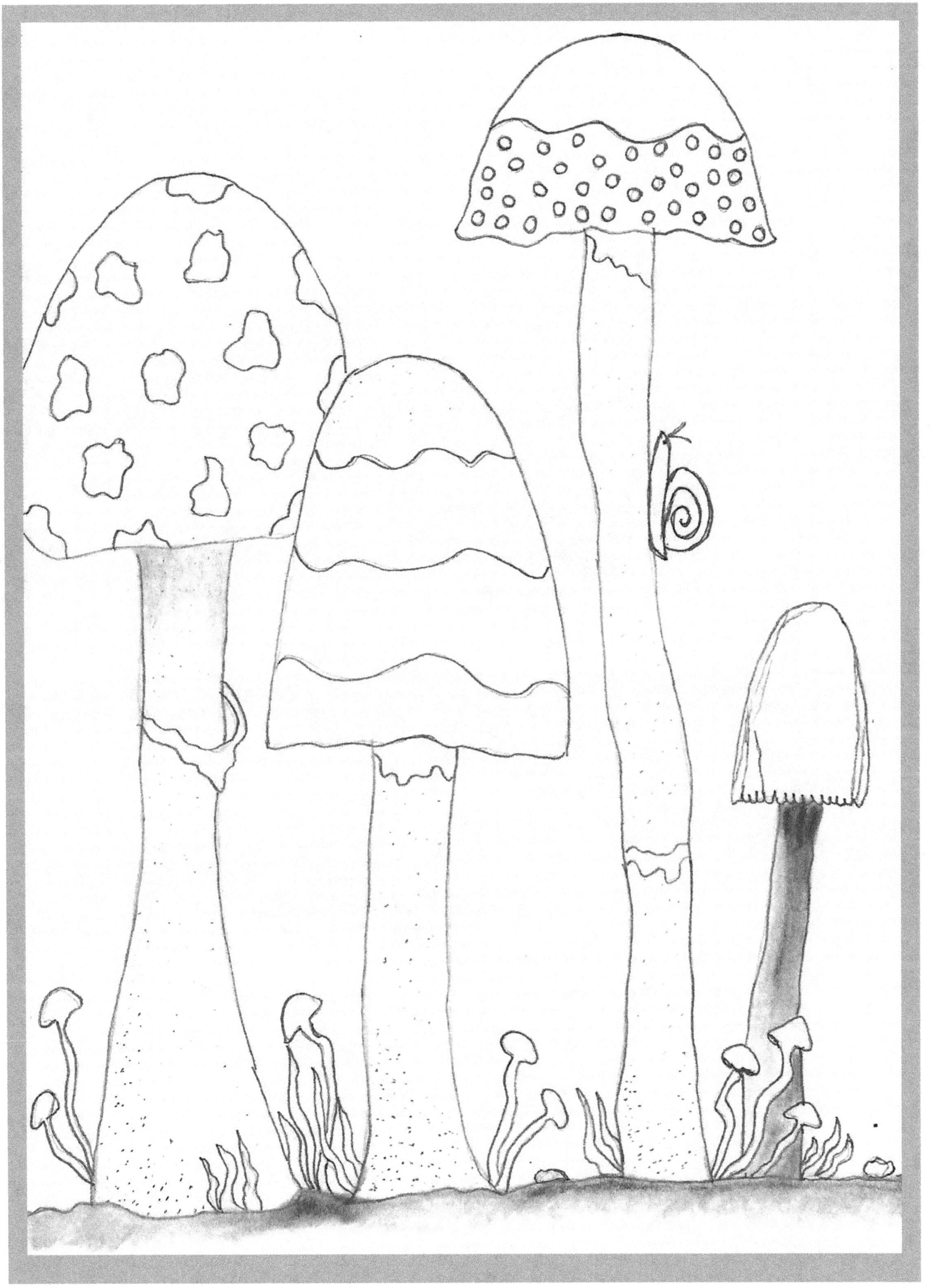

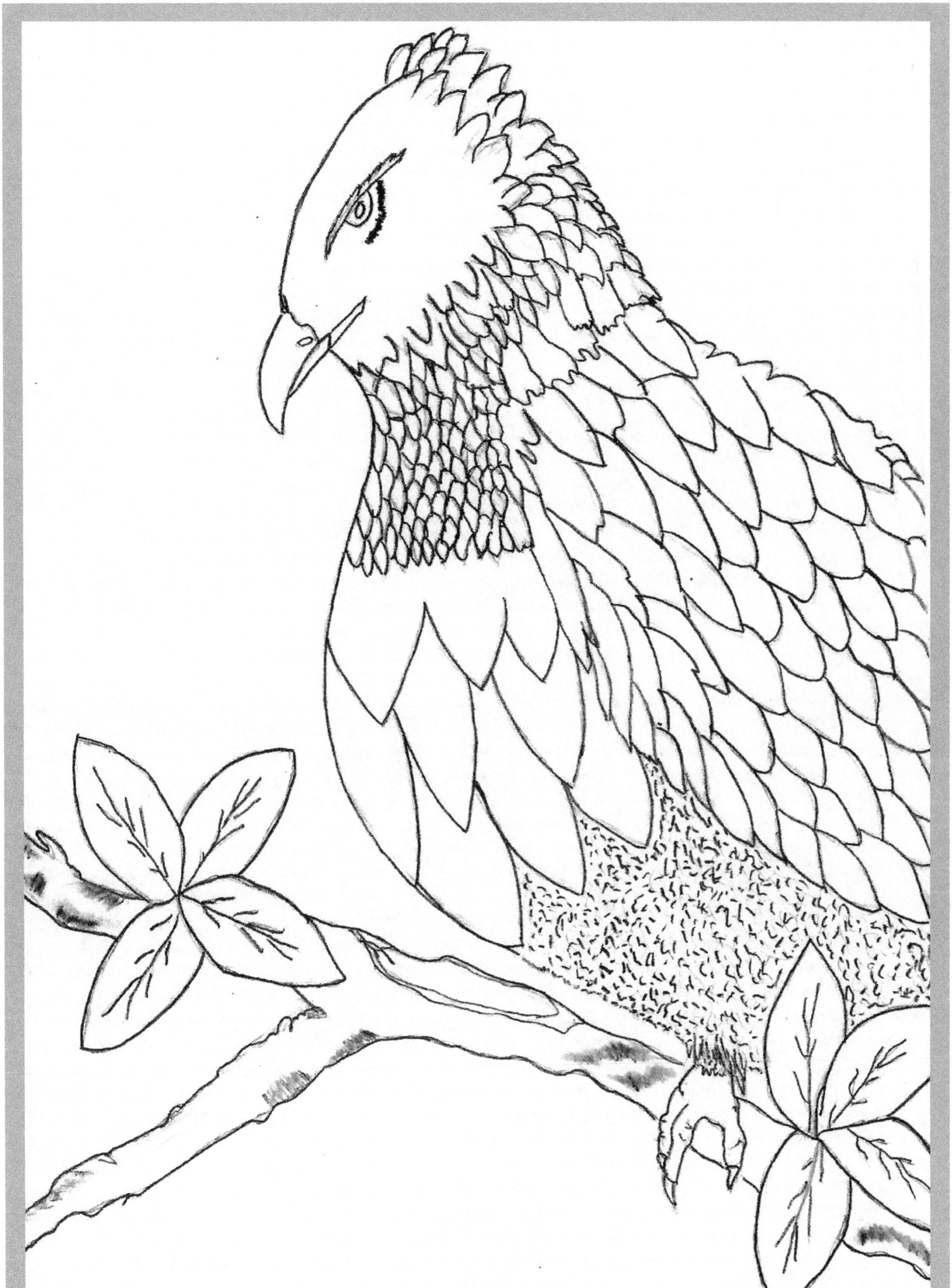

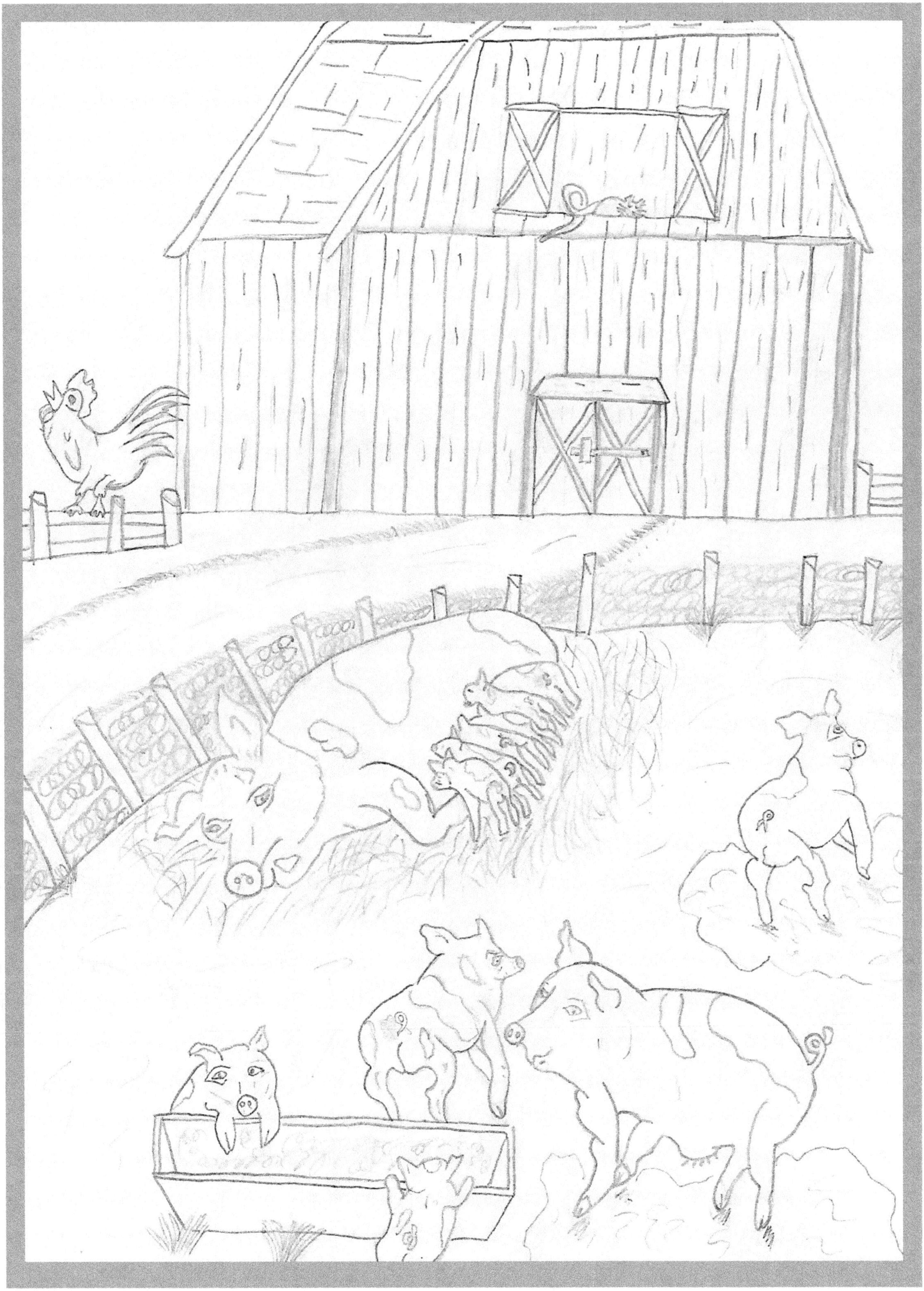

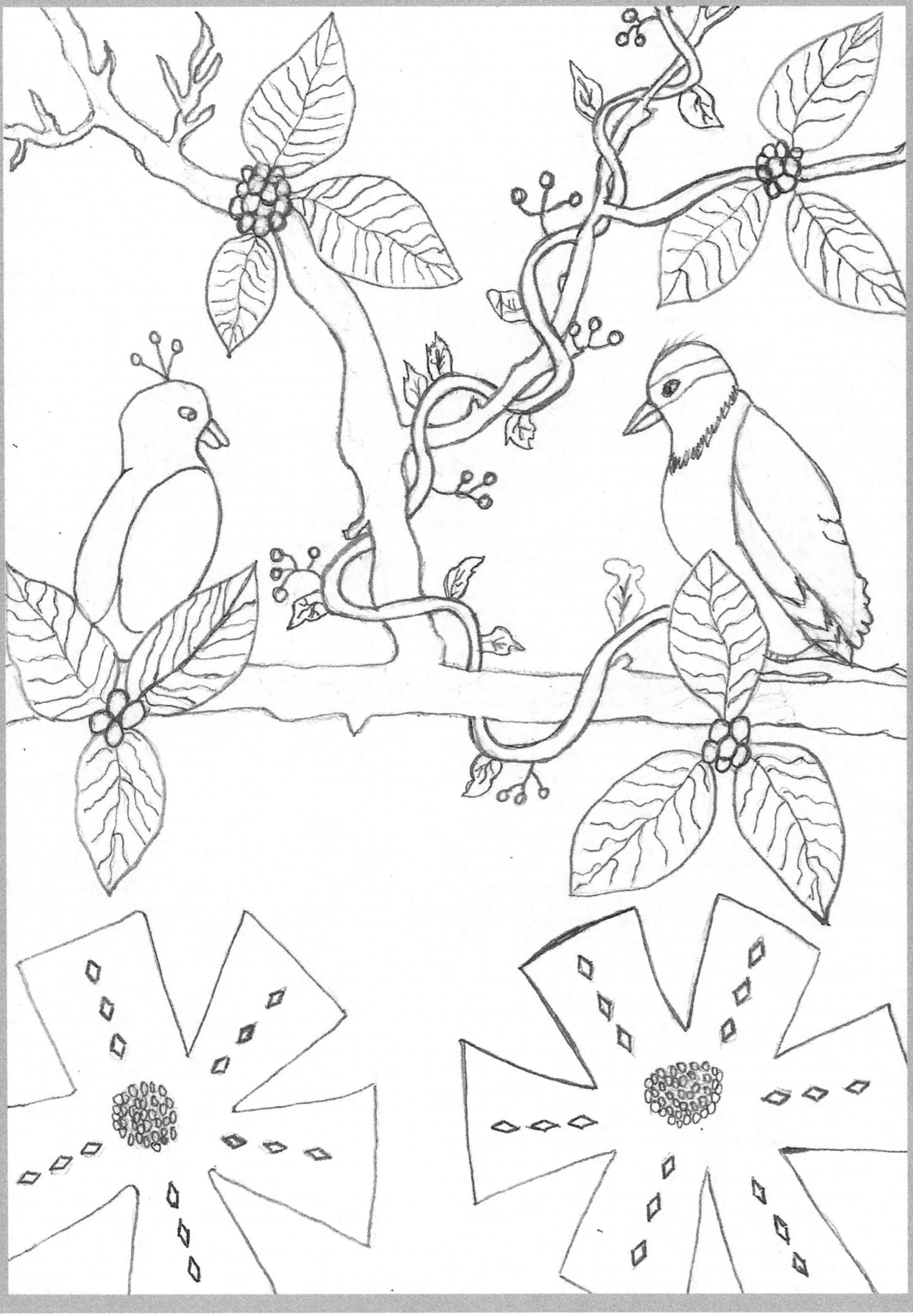

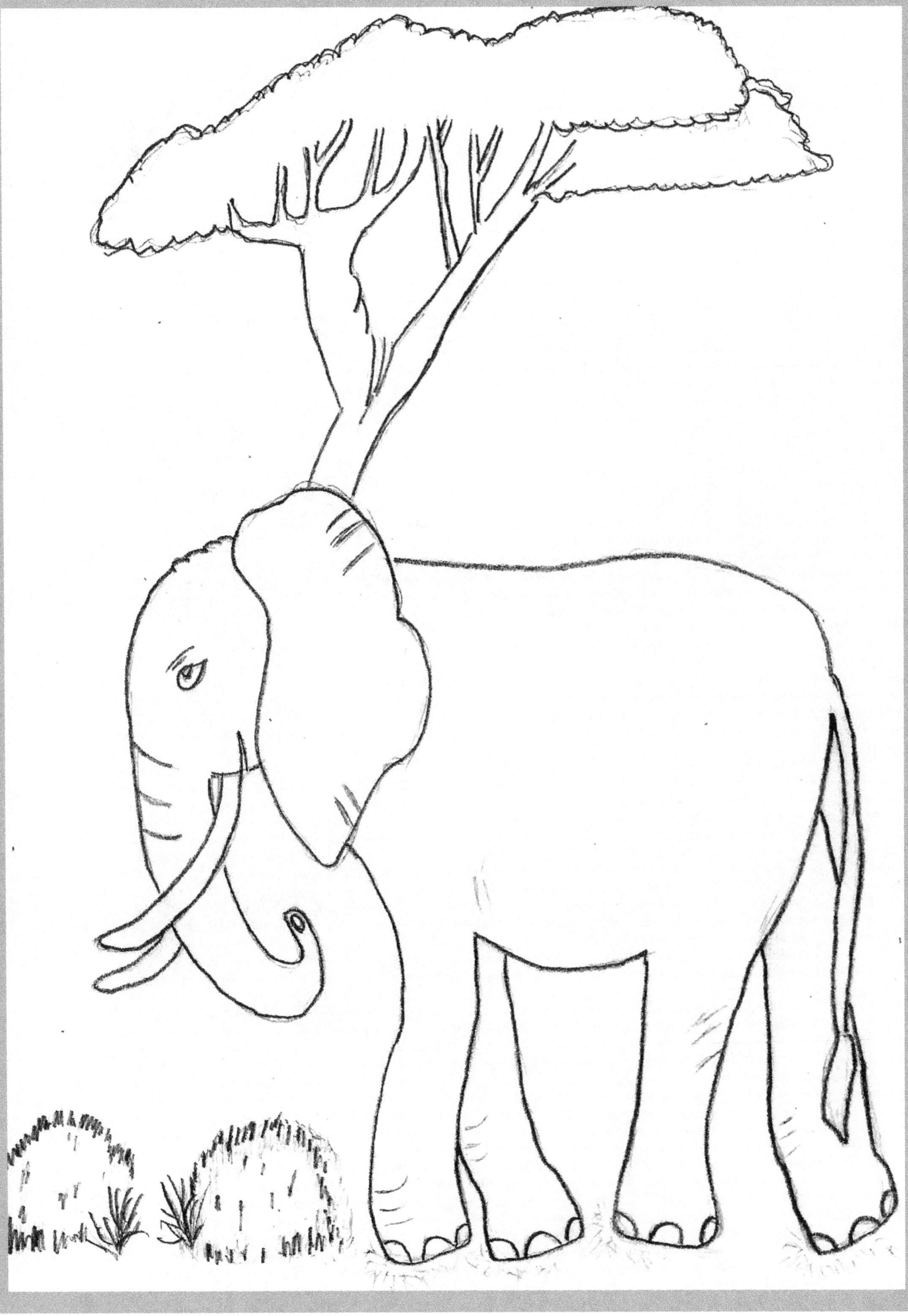

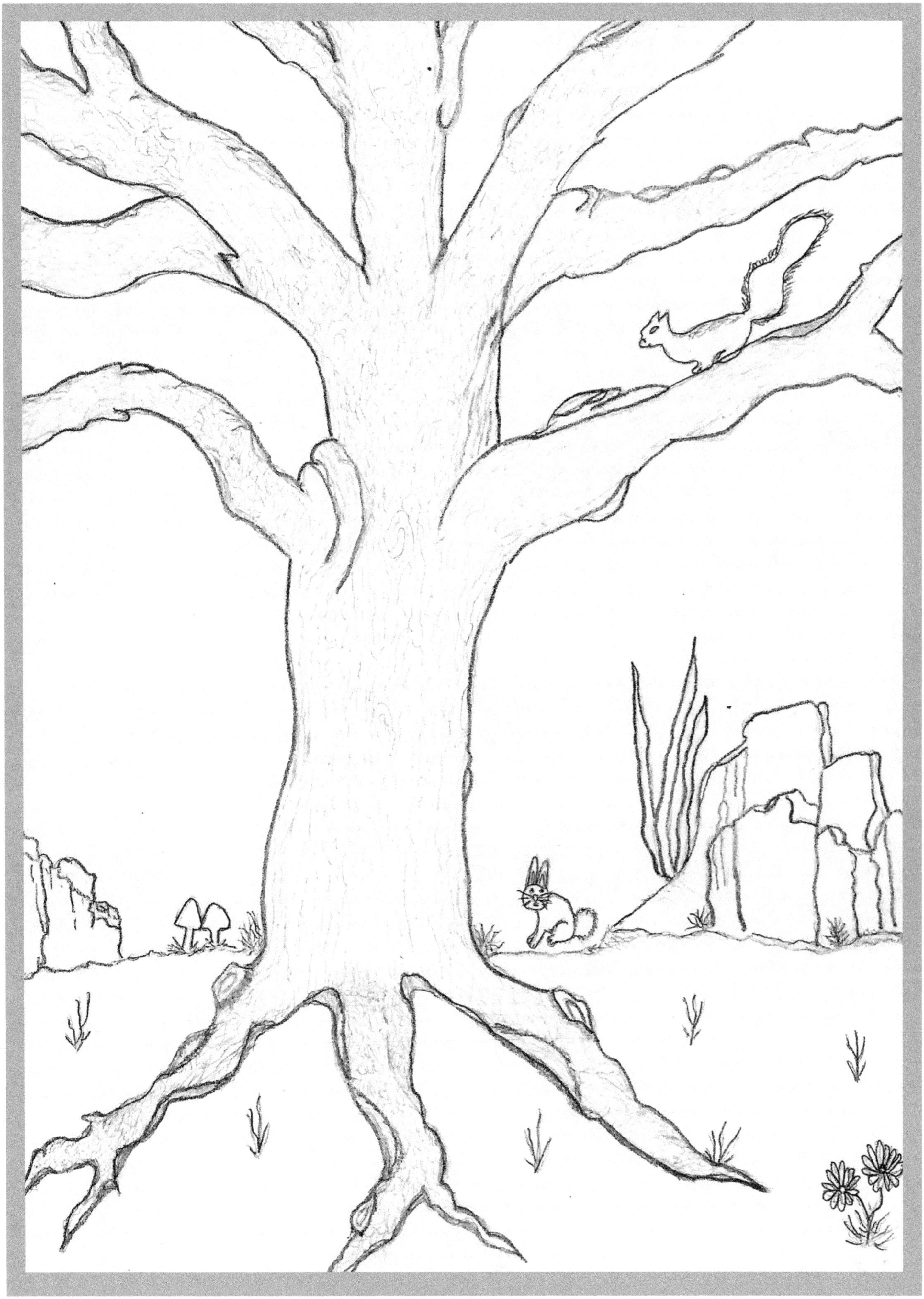

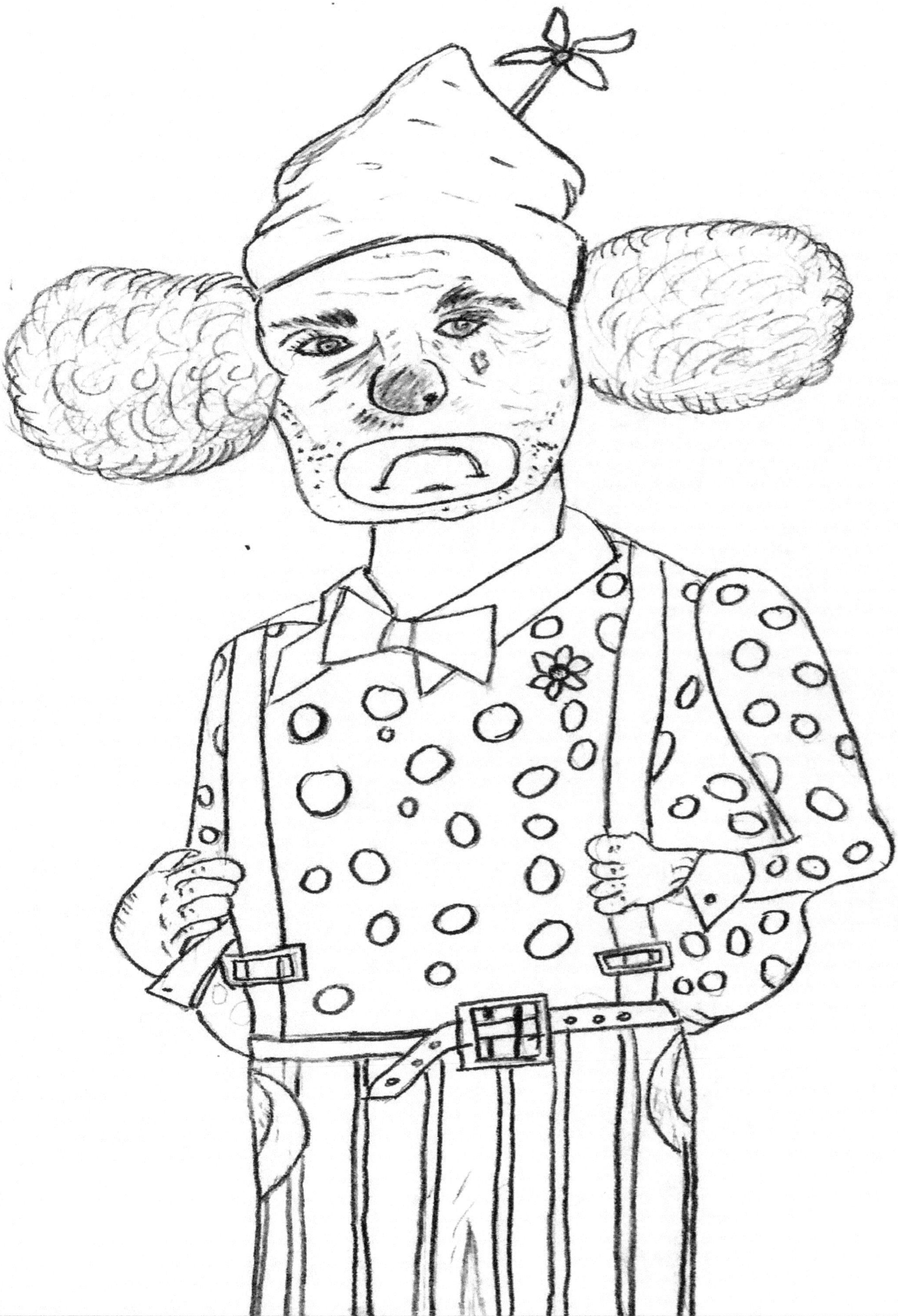

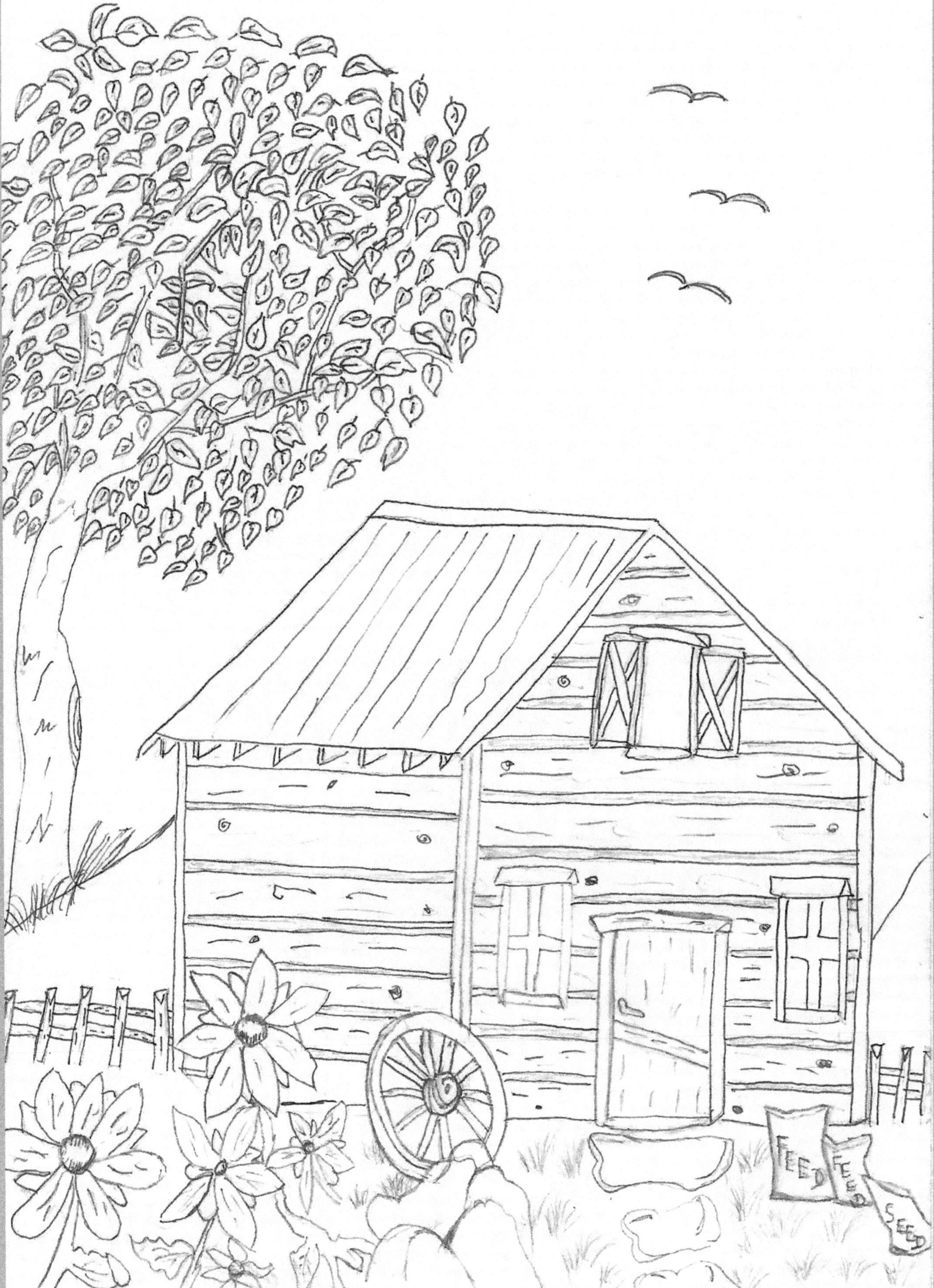
FEED
FEED
SEED

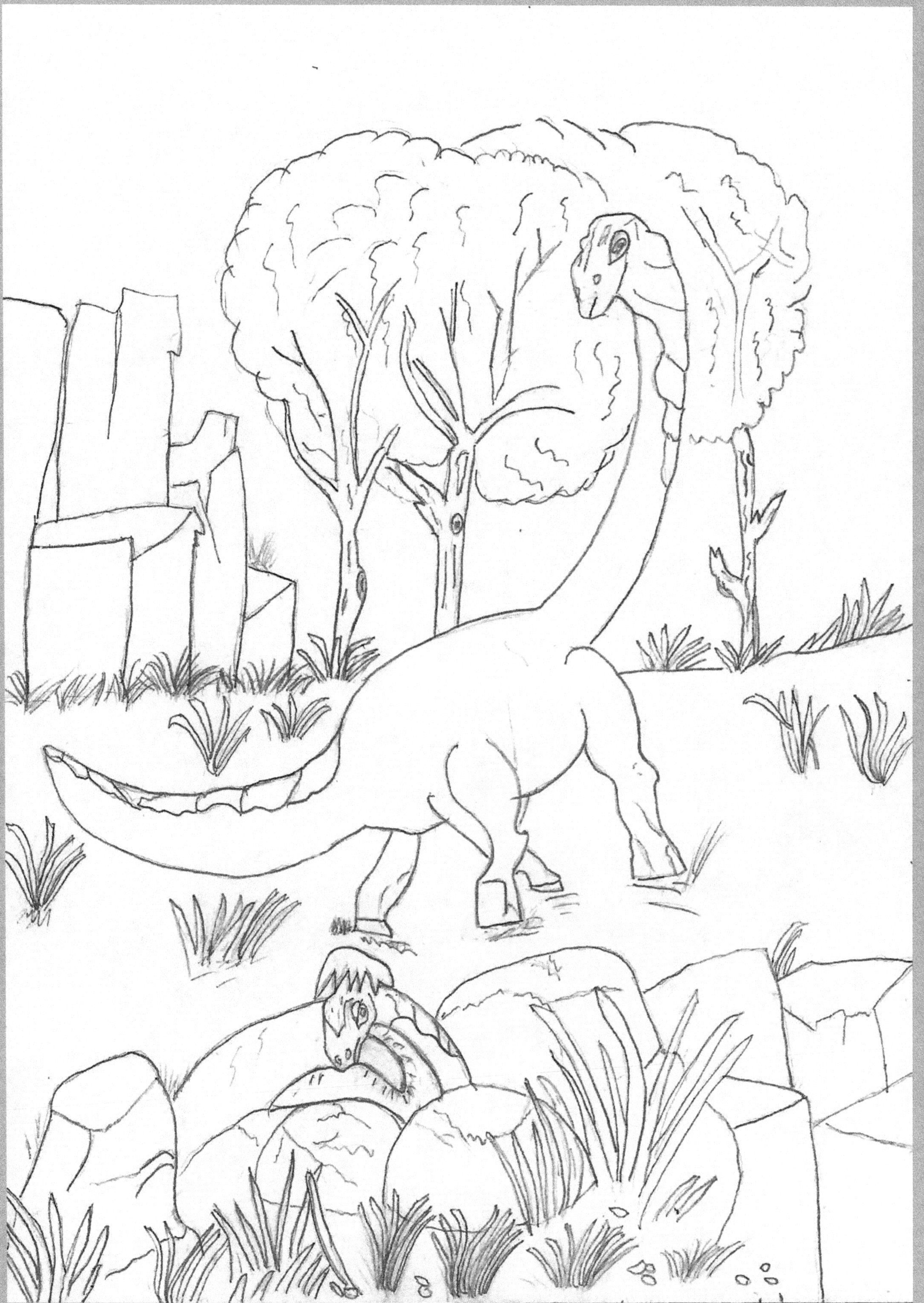

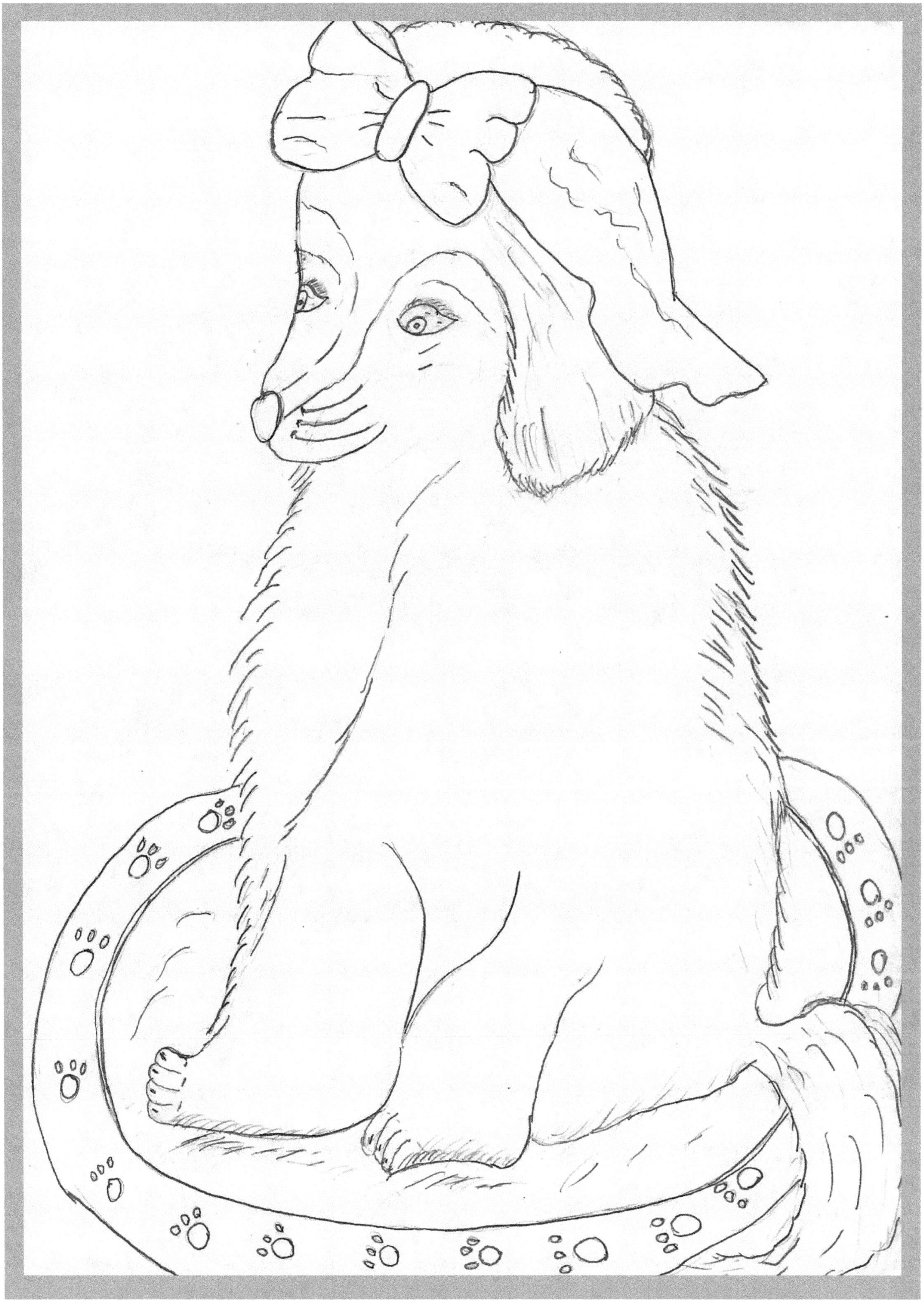

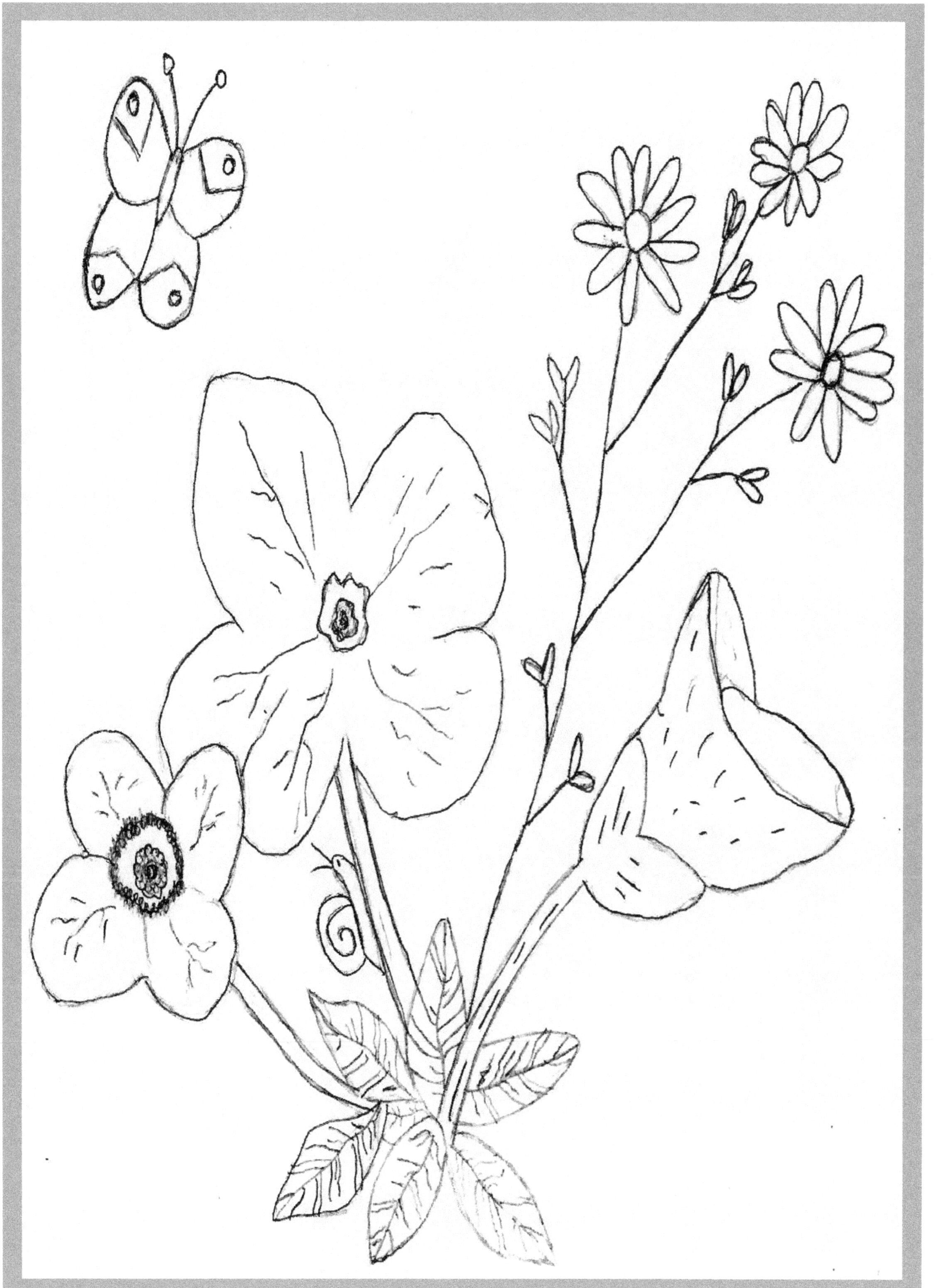

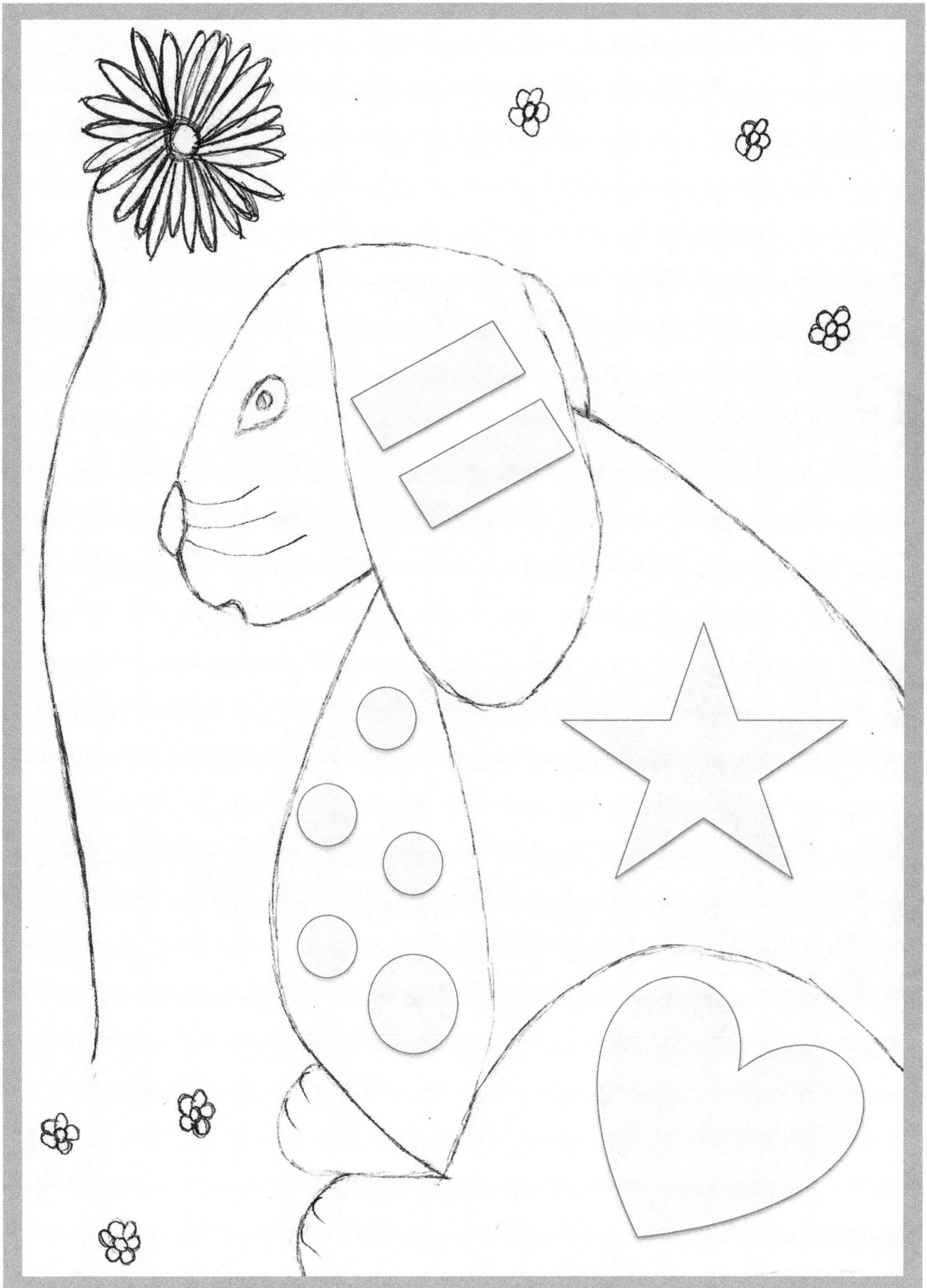

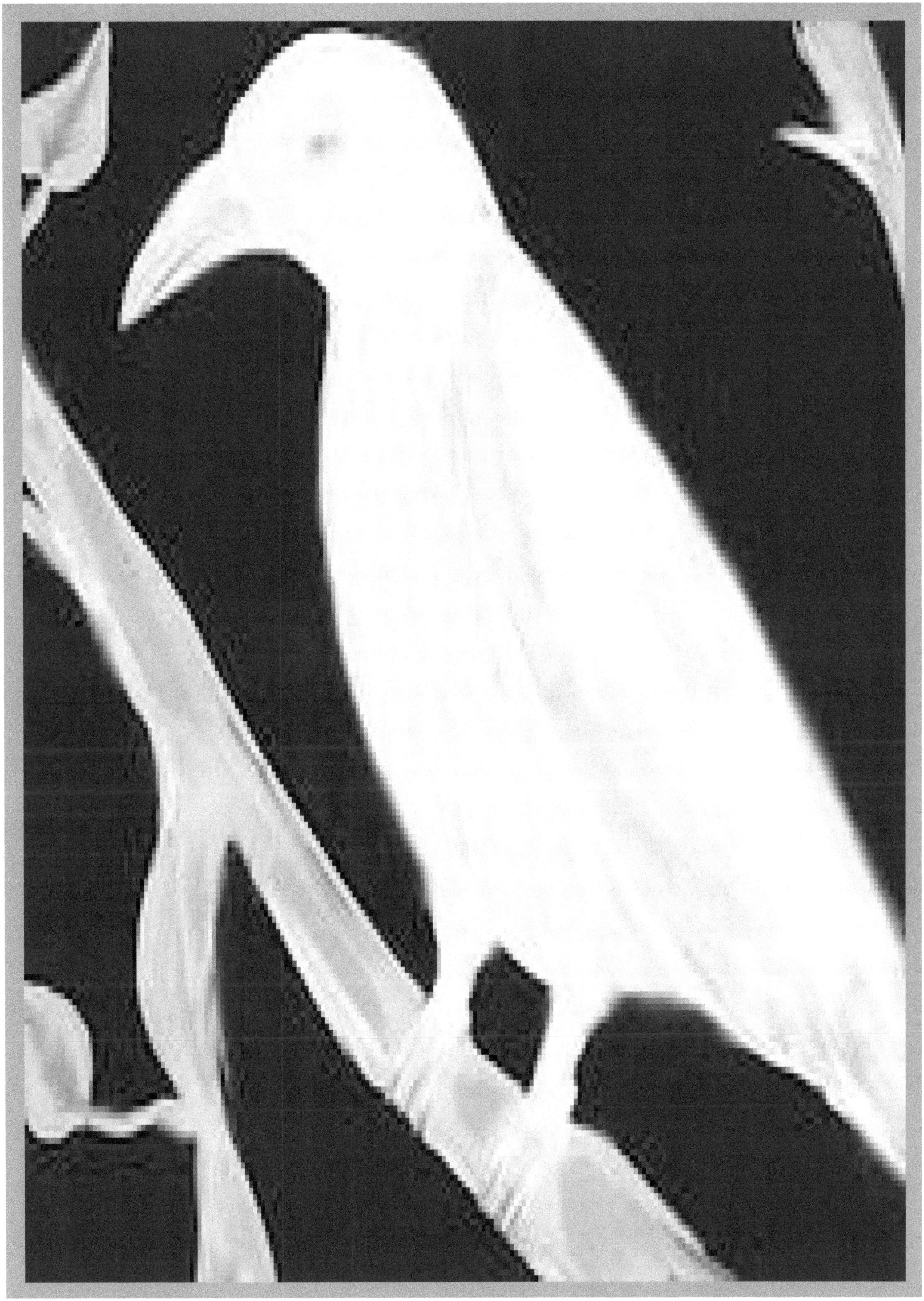

Test Your Colors

www.ingramcontent.com/pod-product-compliance
Lightning Source LLC
Chambersburg PA
CBHW080828170526
45158CB00009B/2540
* 9 7 8 1 0 8 8 4 6 7 8 1 7 *